CAREER EXPLORATION

Automotive Master Mechanic

by Tracey Boraas

Consultants:
Ed Anderson, Mechanical Division Manager
Ken Roberts, Vice President, Communications
Automotive Service Association

CAPSTONE BOOKS
an imprint of Capstone Press
Mankato, Minnesota

Capstone Books are published by Capstone Press
151 Good Counsel Drive, P.O. Box 669, Mankato, Minnesota 56002
http://www.capstone-press.com

Library of Congress Cataloging-in-Publication Data
Boraas, Tracey
    Automotive Master Mechanic/by Tracey Boraas.
    p. cm.—(Career exploration)
    Includes bibliographical references and index.
    Summary: Introduces the career of the automotive master mechanic by
providing information about educational requirements, duties, work place, salary,
employment outlook, and possible future positions.
    ISBN 0-7368-0486-2
    1. Automobiles—Maintenance and repair—Juvenile literature. 2. Automobile
mechanics—Juvenile literature. [1. Automobiles—Maintenance and
repair—Vocational guidance. 2. Automobile mechanics. 3. Vocational guidance.]
I. Title. II. Series.
TL152 .B617 2000
629.28'72'023—dc21   99-053970

Editorial Credits

Connie R. Colwell, editor; Steve Christensen, cover designer; Kia Bielke, production
    designer and illustrator; Heidi Schoof, photo researcher

Photo Credits

FPG International LLC, 14; Michael Krasowitz, 9; C. Reggie Parker, 16;
    Chris Salvo, 22
International Stock, 38, 40; Mark Bolster, 6
Photo Network, 35; Daniel J. McCleery, 10
Photri Microstock, 25; Dennis Mac Donald, 42
SHAFFER PHOTOGRAPHY/James L. Shaffer, cover, 26, 30
Uniphoto, 13, 20; Shaun van Stëyn, 18, 33

1 2 3 4 5 6 05 04 03 02 01 00

Table of Contents

Fast Facts

Career Title	Automotive Master Mechanic
O*NET Number	85302A
DOT Cluster (Dictionary of Occupational Titles)	Machine trades occupations
DOT Number	620.261-010
GOE Number (Guide for Occupational Exploration)	05.05.09
NOC Number (National Occupational Classification-Canada)	732
Salary Range (U.S. Bureau of Labor Statistics and Human Resources Development Canada, late 1990s figures)	U.S.: $13,940 to $100,000 Canada: $16,600 to $55,600 (Canadian dollars)
Minimum Educational Requirements	U.S.: none Canada: four-year apprenticeship
Certification/Licensing Requirements	U.S.: optional Canada: required

Subject Knowledge   Basic electronics and computers;
                             physics; chemistry; English;
                             automotive technology

Personal Abilities/Skills   Understand automobiles; have
                             mechanical ability; analyze data;
                             use good reasoning ability; use
                             various tools; use hands and
                             fingers with skill; lift heavy objects;
                             work in awkward positions; follow
                             safety practices; use
                             communication skills

Job Outlook   U.S.: excellent
                             Canada: fair

Personal Interests   Mechanical: interest in applying
                             mechanical principles to practical
                             situations, using machines, hand
                             tools or techniques

Similar Types of Jobs   Transmission mechanic; diesel
                             truck and bus mechanic;
                             motorcycle mechanic; automotive
                             body repairer; repair service
                             estimator

Chapter 1

Automotive Master Mechanic

Automotive master mechanics work with automobiles such as cars and light trucks. Light trucks include vans and pickups with gasoline engines. Automotive master mechanics inspect and repair these vehicles. They fix or replace parts that are not working properly.

Duties

An automotive master mechanic's main duty is to service automobiles. Mechanics talk with automobile owners. Owners describe problems they are having with their automobiles. Mechanics then write these problems on a repair order. This form lists the problems the owners want fixed.

Automotive master mechanics service automobiles.

7

Automotive master mechanics use hand tools such as wrenches.

powered by electricity. Infrared engine analyzers and computerized diagnostic equipment are electronic service equipment. Infrared engine analyzers use heat waves to locate automobile problems. Computerized diagnostic equipment uses computers to help locate the sources of automobile problems.

Mechanics also use computerized databases to find current information about automobiles. These computer files organize and store information about automobiles. Mechanics use databases to learn about problems common to certain automobiles. They also use databases to learn about new tools and new repair methods.

Most automotive master mechanics must buy their own hand tools. Mechanics should buy the best quality tools that they can afford. The tools must be durable. They must be able to withstand heavy use. Over time, automotive master mechanics may spend between $2,000 and $11,000 on their hand tools. Employers provide mechanics with power tools and electronic service equipment.

Automotive Master Mechanics at Work

Automotive master mechanics work in different settings. Many mechanics work for automotive dealers. These businesses sell new and used cars. Some automotive master mechanics work for automotive repair shops. Others work for automotive service centers in discount or department stores. Still others own their own automotive repair businesses.

Automotive master mechanics usually work 40 hours per week. They do not always work daytime shifts. Automotive repair shops often are open during hours that are convenient for their customers. Some mechanics may work evening or weekend shifts. They may work overtime to finish jobs.

Specialists and Certification

Automotive master mechanics may specialize in repairing different parts of automobiles. For example, some specialize in transmission systems. Transmission specialists are experts on the gears that send power from the engine to the wheels. Other mechanics specialize in brake systems. Still others become engine performance specialists. These experts test and repair engines. Specialties may require one to two years of extra training and experience.

Automotive master mechanics may choose to become certified. Mechanics in the United States can take tests in eight specialty areas. They must be highly skilled and experienced. Mechanics who pass all eight tests earn the title of certified master automotive technician. In Canada, mechanics also may earn certification by completing a four-year training program.

Automotive master mechanics may specialize in repairing different parts of automobiles.

Chapter 2

Day-to-Day Activities

Most automotive master mechanics perform some of the same basic duties each day. Their other duties vary depending on their work settings, skills, and experience.

Automotive Dealerships

Automotive master mechanics may work in service shops of automotive dealerships. People buy automobiles at automotive dealerships. Dealerships often have service departments for the types of automobiles they sell. These shops keep parts in stock for these types of automobiles. Mechanics who work in these shops often have special training in repairing these automobiles.

Automotive master mechanics may work in automotive dealerships.

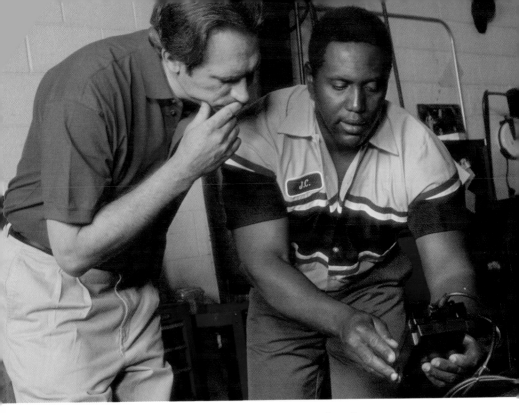

Service advisors talk to customers about automobile problems.

Most automotive dealerships have service advisors and service managers. Service advisors talk to customers about automobile problems. They write repair orders to tell the mechanics what the customers want fixed.

Service managers supervise automotive master mechanics. Service managers assign one to two cars to each mechanic. Mechanics then determine what is wrong with their assigned automobiles.

Mechanics sometimes need more specific information about the customers' automobile problems. Service advisors may contact the customers for this information.

Automotive master mechanics tell service advisors what repairs automobiles need. Service advisors then contact customers for permission to perform the suggested repairs.

Mechanics drive the automobiles into work areas called bays. Mechanics then perform the necessary repairs. Mechanics sometimes keep automobiles overnight or for several days. Mechanics may need this time to make repairs or to order parts.

Mechanics in automotive dealership service shops usually work 40 to 45 hours per week. They sometimes work more hours in order to complete repair jobs. They also may work weekend or evening shifts.

Automotive master mechanics often specialize in certain automotive services.

Retail Automotive Service Centers

Some automotive master mechanics work in retail automotive service centers. These repair shops often are franchises. A company gives these businesses permission to sell the company's products or services. Franchises are sometimes called chain stores. Franchises may have stores in several cities, states, or provinces.

Retail automotive service centers often specialize in a few types of automobile services. These services usually involve maintenance and simple repairs. These may include oil changes, muffler replacement, and tire repair. Their mechanics have the special training and equipment needed to quickly perform these services.

Mechanics at retail automotive service centers must be able to work well under pressure. These centers make money by servicing a large number of automobiles each day. Mechanics must service automobiles quickly and accurately. Customers at these centers usually do not need appointments. Customers often drive in with their automobiles and wait while mechanics complete the jobs.

Some independent shop owners hire other mechanics to help them.

Independent Automotive Repair Shops

Some automotive master mechanics own independent automotive repair shops. These shops are not part of dealerships or franchises. These independent shops are privately owned.

Independent automotive repair shops often are small. The owner may be the shop's only automotive mechanic. Owners often work more than 40 hours per week. Some independent automotive repair shop owners are able to hire other mechanics. This is usually after they have been in business for several years. These shops have many customers and perform many services. They then can afford to hire more automotive master mechanics.

Chapter 3

The Right Candidate

Automotive master mechanics need a variety of interests and skills. Mechanics should have an interest in machines and tools. They should enjoy working with their hands. They also must be able to make quick, accurate decisions.

What Mechanics Need to Know

Automotive master mechanics must have certain skills and abilities. They must know how automobiles work. They should understand what causes automotive problems. They also must be able to work with tools and machines.

Automotive master mechanics need strong computer and electronics skills. Computers now control many automobile parts. These parts include engines and radios. Electronics are used in brakes and many other automobile parts.

Automotive master mechanics must understand how automobiles work.

Abilities and Interests

Automotive master mechanics must have strong mechanical skills. They must be able to work with machines. Mechanics must be able to use various tools to adjust and repair automobile parts.

Automotive master mechanics must have good reasoning and decision-making skills. Mechanics must be able to correctly determine automobile problems and know how to fix them.

Automotive master mechanics must be physically fit. They often stand for long periods of time. Automotive master mechanics lean over engines. They lie on their backs under cars. They lift heavy automobile parts and tools. They often work in cramped spaces. Automotive master mechanics must bend and twist their bodies. They do much of their work standing, kneeling, or crouching. They are on their feet much of the day.

Mechanics must be able to handle stress. They often work long hours. They may be under pressure to service a large number of

Automotive master mechanics should be physically fit.

automobiles each day. They sometimes must deal with dissatisfied customers. They often work in noisy surroundings. They must perform their jobs quickly and accurately in spite of these stressful factors.

Automotive master mechanics must be careful. They must follow safety practices to avoid injuries. They must keep work areas neat

Automotive master mechanics must carefully work with tools.

and clean to avoid slips and spills. They must carefully lift heavy parts. They must carefully work with dangerous tools and equipment. Some automobile parts and tools may be hot or sharp. Minor cuts, burns, and bruises are common. Mechanics who follow safety procedures decrease their chances of injuries.

Basic Skills

Automotive master mechanics must know how to use different types of tools and equipment. They use jacks and hoists. These tools lift automobiles and engines so that mechanics can work on parts on the automobiles' undersides. Mechanics use power tools such as pneumatic wrenches. These wrenches use compressed air to remove bolts quickly. Automotive master mechanics also use common hand tools such as screwdrivers and wrenches. Mechanics use these tools to work on small parts.

Mechanics must understand basic electronics and computers. Newer cars contain between 10 and 15 parts operated by computer. Some engine parts and dashboard instruments are electronic systems. Brakes, transmissions, and steering systems also are electronic.

Automotive master mechanics must have strong communication skills. They must

Skills

Workplace Skills   Yes / No

Resources:
Assign use of time . . . . ☑ ☐
Assign use of money . . . . ☐ ☑
Assign use of material and facility resources . . . . ☑ ☐
Assign use of human resources . . . . ☐ ☑

Interpersonal Skills:
Take part as a member of a team . . . . ☑ ☐
Teach others . . . . ☑ ☐
Serve clients/customers . . . . ☑ ☐
Show leadership . . . . ☑ ☐
Work with others to arrive at a decision . . . . ☑ ☐
Work with a variety of people . . . . ☑ ☐

Information:
Acquire and judge information . . . . ☑ ☐
Understand and follow legal requirements . . . . ☑ ☐
Organize and maintain information . . . . ☑ ☐
Understand and communicate information . . . . ☑ ☐
Use computers to process information . . . . ☑ ☐

Systems:
Identify, understand, and work with systems . . . . ☑ ☐
Understand environmental, social, political, economic,
    or business systems . . . . ☐ ☑
Oversee and correct system performance . . . . ☑ ☐
Improve and create systems . . . . ☐ ☑

Technology:
Select technology . . . . ☑ ☐
Apply technology to task . . . . ☑ ☐
Maintain and troubleshoot technology . . . . ☑ ☐

Foundation Skills

Basic Skills:
Read . . . . ☑ ☐
Write . . . . ☑ ☐
Do arithmetic and math . . . . ☑ ☐
Speak and listen . . . . ☑ ☐

Thinking Skills:
Learn . . . . ☑ ☐
Reason . . . . ☑ ☐
Think creatively . . . . ☑ ☐
Make decisions . . . . ☑ ☐
Solve problems . . . . ☑ ☐

Personal Qualities:
Take individual responsibility . . . . ☑ ☐
Have self-esteem and self-management . . . . ☑ ☐
Be sociable . . . . ☑ ☐
Be fair, honest, and sincere . . . . ☑ ☐

listen carefully to customers as they explain their automobile problems. Mechanics also must have good speaking skills. They must speak clearly with customers and co-workers. Mechanics also may need to communicate with other mechanics or supervisors in writing. They must be willing to study technical manuals. These books contain detailed information about particular types of automobiles.

Chapter 4

Preparing for the Career

People must complete appropriate training to become automotive master mechanics. Some mechanics learn their trade through apprenticeship programs. Apprentices receive training on the job. Other mechanics complete automotive mechanic programs at community colleges, vocational schools, or technical schools.

High School Education

Students can prepare for careers in automotive mechanics while they are in high school. They should take classes in electronics, science, and computers. These classes teach students how various machines work. Classes in English and

Students who want to become automotive master mechanics should take classes in electronics.

communications also are helpful. These classes help students learn to communicate with others.

Many high schools offer automotive training programs. Some of these programs are basic introductions to automotive mechanics. Other programs prepare students for jobs as trainee mechanics after graduation.

In Canada, high school students can enter an apprenticeship program. These students must be in grade 10 or higher. They earn high school credits through the Registered Apprenticeship Program (RAP) as they train. Students can complete their apprenticeship programs after graduation from high school.

Apprenticeship

In Canada, people must complete four years of apprenticeship before they can become journeyman mechanics. Journeyman mechanics are highly skilled and experienced mechanics. They can work in all automotive service areas.

Automotive mechanic apprentices work four 12-month periods. Each period includes 10 months of hands-on training under the employer's supervision. Apprentices then complete two months of classroom instruction.

Apprentices earn money while they train and learn.

Apprentices earn money while they train. They may earn about 55 percent of the average technician wage during the first year. They may earn as much as 90 percent by the fourth year.

Apprentices take a final exam at the end of the four-year apprenticeship period. Apprentices are certified as journeyman mechanics after passing this exam. Provincial governments give these exams.

Post-Secondary Education

Many people interested in the automotive field complete a formal post-secondary program. They may complete training at community colleges, vocational schools, and technical schools.

Formal automotive mechanic programs vary. Some programs provide training only in automotive mechanics. Some automotive programs take only six months to a year to complete.

It usually takes two years to complete an automotive mechanics program at a community college. These programs include classes and hands-on practice in automobile service. They also include classes in English, math, computers, and electronics.

Community college programs award a two-year certificate or degree at the end of these programs. Students who complete these programs earn an associate's degree.

On-the-Job Training

Some automotive master mechanics learn on the job. In the United States, people can work as mechanics without completing any formal training. These mechanics learn by assisting and working with experienced mechanics on the job.

Formal automotive mechanic programs include hands-on practice in automotive service.

Some automobile manufacturers and dealers have training programs for mechanics. They provide instructors and equipment. They also provide current models of automobiles on which students practice. Students spend time in class. They also work in the dealers' service departments. They work with experienced mechanics.

Employers usually prefer formal training programs to on-the-job training. Today's

High School Diploma ➤

Apprenticeship (Canada) ➤

automobiles are much more complex than those of the past. They contain computer and electronic systems. Employers need mechanics skilled in repairing and maintaining these systems.

Certification

In the United States, mechanics who pass tests to become certified are called certified master automotive technicians. These technicians must prove they have knowledge and experience in eight service areas. These areas include engine repair, transmission repair, and brake systems. Drive line repair, suspension/steering repair, and engine performance also are service areas. Drive line repair includes repair of the tires and the axles around which the wheels turn. Suspension/steering repair includes repair of the parts that support automobiles and the parts that control the movement of the tires. Electrical repair and heating/air conditioning repair are other service areas.

On-the-Job Training/ Formal Education → **Certification (Optional)** →

In the United States, the National Institute of Automotive Service Excellence (ASE) certifies mechanics. Certification can help mechanics earn more money or gain more responsibilities. To become certified, mechanics must have at least two years of experience in an area of automotive repair. They must pass a written test in that area. They become certified master automotive technicians when they have passed all eight tests. Certified master automotive technicians must retake and pass these tests every five years.

Automotive mechanics in Canada are certified as journeyman mechanics by their province's government. This certification covers all automotive service areas. Journeyman mechanics may receive ASE certification. But journeyman certification is so highly regarded that few technicians get ASE certification. Journeyman mechanics also may choose to get interprovincial trade certification. This certification allows them to work in any province in Canada.

Chapter 5

The Market

Automotive master mechanics have their choice of several work settings. They may advance into other jobs in the automotive industry. They also may work in related careers.

Employment Projections

Automobiles continue to become more complex. Automotive master mechanics will continue to be in demand in the United States and Canada. Mechanic jobs are expected to increase in the United States. The market is expected to remain fair for those entering the field in Canada.

Automotive master mechanics with electronics skills have the best chance to get jobs. Mechanics who lack formal training are likely to have more difficulty competing for jobs.

Automotive master mechanics will continue to be in demand in the United States and Canada.

Experienced automotive master mechanics can advance by becoming specialists.

Many automotive master mechanics are expected to retire in the coming years. Their jobs will need to be filled. This field will continue to need large numbers of new workers each year.

Salary and Benefits

Mechanics' salaries vary depending on employers and experience. The average mechanic in the United States earns between $13,940 and $44,200 per year. In Canada, mechanics earn between $16,600 and $55,600 per year.

Some certified master automotive technicians employed by automotive dealerships and independent repair shops receive commissions. These mechanics are paid based on how much work they do. They also are paid based on how much money the service center makes. Service centers make more money when mechanics complete many jobs and perform them well. Master mechanics who work on commission can earn from $70,000 to $100,000 per year.

Automotive master mechanics may receive benefits such as paid vacation, sick days, and health insurance. Mechanics who work at dealerships or retail service centers are more likely to receive benefits. Small independent shops may not offer these benefits.

Advancement Opportunities

Experienced automotive master mechanics can advance by becoming specialists. These people are experts in certain areas of automotive care. Experienced mechanics also may become supervisors if they have leadership skills. They may become service managers.

Some experienced automotive master mechanics may open their own repair shops. They then may hire mechanics to work for them.

Automotive master mechanics who enjoy working with customers may become automotive service repair estimators. These people calculate how much it will cost to fix automobiles. They give customers estimates of the recommended repairs before mechanics start their work.

Related Careers

People who are interested in the automotive industry can work in related careers. They can repair diesel trucks and buses. These vehicles have different engines than automobiles. They also can repair motorcycles. People interested in automobiles also can work in auto body shops. Workers in these shops paint automobiles or repair automobiles that have been damaged in accidents.

People will continue to rely on automobiles for transportation. Automotive master mechanics are needed to maintain and repair these automobiles now and in the future.

People who are interested in the automotive industry can work in auto body shops.

Words to Know

apprentice (uh-PREN-tiss)—someone who learns a trade or craft by working with a skilled person

bay (BAY)—a separated work space in a larger, enclosed area

database (DAY-tuh-bayss)—computer files that organize and store information

hoist (HOIST)—a piece of equipment used for lifting heavy objects

lathe (LAYTH)—a machine that holds a piece of wood or metal while turning it against a cutting tool that shapes it

transmission (transs-MISH-uhn)—a series of gears that send power from the engine to the wheels

To Learn More

Cosgrove, Holli, ed. *Career Discovery Encyclopedia.* Vol. 1. Chicago: Ferguson Publishing, 2000.

Lee, Richard S. and Mary Price Lee. *Careers for Car Buffs and Other Freewheeling Types.* VGM Careers for You. Lincolnwood, Ill.: VGM Career Horizons, 1997.

Weber, Robert M. *Opportunities in Automotive Service Careers.* VGM Opportunities. Lincolnwood, Ill.: VGM Career Horizons, 1997.

Useful Addresses

Automotive Service Association
P.O. Box 929
Bedford, TX 76095-0929

**Canadian Automotive Repair and Service
Council (CARS)**
9121 Leslie Street
Number 6
Richmond Hill, ON L4B 3J9
Canada

**National Institute for Automotive Service
Excellence**
13505 Dulles Technology Drive
Suite 2
Herndon, VA 20171-3421

Internet Sites

Automotive Learning Online
http://www.innerbody.com/innerauto/htm/auto.
html

Motor Vehicle Mechanics
http://www.hrdc-drhc.gc.ca/JobFutures/english/
volume1/732/732.htm

**National Institute for Automotive Service
Excellence**
http://www.asecert.org

**Occupational Outlook Handbook—
Automotive Mechanics**
http://stats.bls.gov/oco/ocos181.htm

Index